THE BEST WORDS FROM A-Z

A Guide to Using Positive Words Each Week
to Enhance Your Life and Work

by Gini Graham Scott, Ph.D.

THE BEST WORDS FROM A-Z

Copyright © 2018 by Gini Graham Scott

All rights reserved. No part of this book may be used or reproduced by any means, graphic, electronic, or mechanical, including photocopying, recording, taping or by any information storage retrieval system without the written permission of the author except in the case of brief quotations embodied in critical articles and reviews.

TABLE OF CONTENTS

INTRODUCTION 5
HOW TO USE THIS BOOK.. 7
WEEK 1: 9
WEEK 2: 11
WEEK 3: 13
WEEK 4: 15
WEEK 5: 17
WEEK 6: 19
WEEK 7: 21
WEEK 8: 23
WEEK 9: 25
WEEK 10: 27
WEEK 11: 29
WEEK 12: 31
WEEK 13: 33
1ST QUARTER: IDEAS AND INSIGHTS: 35
WEEK 14: 37
WEEK 15: 39
WEEK 16: 41
WEEK 17: 43
WEEK 18: 45
WEEK 19: 47
WEEK 20: 49
WEEK 21: 51
WEEK 22: 53
WEEK 23: 55
WEEK 24: 57
WEEK 25: 59
WEEK 26: 61
2ND QUARTER: IDEAS AND INSIGHTS: 63
WEEK 27: 65
WEEK 28: 67
WEEK 29: 69
WEEK 30: 71
WEEK 31: 73
WEEK 32: 75

- WEEK 33: 77
- WEEK 34: 79
- WEEK 35: 81
- WEEK 36: 83
- WEEK 37: 85
- WEEK 38: 87
- WEEK 39: 89
- 3RD QUARTER: IDEAS AND INSIGHTS 91
- WEEK 40: 93
- WEEK 41: 95
- WEEK 42: 97
- WEEK 43: 99
- WEEK 44: 101
- WEEK 45: 103
- WEEK 46: 105
- WEEK 47: 107
- WEEK 48: 109
- WEEK 49: 111
- WEEK 50: 113
- WEEK 51: 115
- WEEK 52: 117
- 4TH QUARTER: IDEAS AND INSIGHTS 119
- A YEAR FROM A-Z: IDEAS AND INSIGHTS 121
- ABOUT THE AUTHOR 125

INTRODUCTION

Words can be very powerful.

There are hundreds of quotes about the power of words. The ancient Greek philosopher Socrates says: "The beginning of wisdom is the definition of terms." Motivational speaker Zig Ziglar comments: "There is power in words. What you say is what you get." Spiritual teacher Deepak Chopra notes: "Language creates reality. Words have power. Speak always to create joy." To take one more quote, Frederick Buechner, an American writer and theologian, says: "Words have the power to make things happen."

The Best Words from A-Z has been written in this spirit. It provides a system where you can focus on different positive words each week for a year, in order to think about how to incorporate the power of these words into your life.

To this end, the book features 104 positive words, starting with the letter A, so you can think about two positive words each week. You can divide up how to think about them in various ways. You can focus on both words and imagine how they might work together. You might think about one in the morning and one at night. Or think of one word for three days, the other for the next three days, and both on the seventh day. Or reflect on your insights from thinking about these words for the past week.

The words selected for *The Best Words* come from the first positive words I thought about in deciding what words to choose starting with the letter A until I came up with all the words from A to Z. I selected words that refer to different actions and qualities that contribute to success in life, and you are free to add or substitute your own words each week. Reflect on the chosen words and how they might contribute to improving your everyday life or work.

The idea for this book comes from a private business networking group on Facebook I belong to. Shortly before New Year's, one of the women invited us to contribute an inspirational word starting with the letter of our name. She suggested that we think about that word and how we could get inspiration from it. I missed her instruction to use the first letter of our name, so the first word I posted was "Positive." When the woman pointed out that I should my first name, I came up with "Gratitude" and began to think of other G words, coming up with "Glory" and "Greatness." Then, I began thinking of many other positive words. After I had come up with three dozen words, I thought about applying them over a period of time, and then about organizing them according to types of words or time. Finally, I realized how all these words fit nicely into a 52 weeks' time frame for using these words in one's life, and so *The Best Words from A-Z* was born.

HOW TO USE THIS BOOK

This book is divided into 52 sections -- one for each week. The beginning of the section lists two words which you can reflect on together or separately in any order. As already noted, you can think of one in the morning, the other at night; or you can think of one for the first three days, the other for the next three days, and use the seventh day to think about how the two words have influenced or affected your week. Or reflect on both words on the seventh day. You can also add in or substitute your own words or change the order of the words, though this book is designed for you to go from A to Z.

Following the two words there is a section for your notes. As you reflect on the words, you can write down your thoughts immediately, or later record your observations on how the words affected your day or what you learned by thinking about each word. Or when you first think about the words, consider what that tells you about yourself or what lesson you might learn. Should you need more space for your thoughts, add an extra page. Or create a journal to reflect on your word or words each day. And if you prefer, record your thoughts on a recording device.

At the end of each 13 week period or quarter, there is a section for you to reflect on what you have learned or how you have been affected by these words each week. At the end of the year, reflect on what you have gained from the experience. Additionally, during these periods of reflection, add whatever comes to mind. Should you get any inspiration for new projects or ventures, include them in your reflections.

So now, start thinking about your first two words and draw on their power to inspire you and change your life for the very best.

WEEK 1:

Your words:

ACHIEVE

ATTAIN

INSIGHTS FROM MY WORDS

WEEK 2:

Your words:

ABUNDANCE

ACKNOWLEDGMENT

INSIGHTS FROM MY WORDS

WEEK 3:

Your words:

ABILITY

ACCOMPLISHMENT

INSIGHTS FROM MY WORDS

WEEK 4:

Your words:

BRAVE

BOUNTIFUL

INSIGHTS FROM MY WORDS

WEEK 5:

Your words:

BEST

BEAUTY

INSIGHTS FROM MY WORDS

WEEK 6:

Your words:

COURAGE

CHOICE

INSIGHTS FROM MY WORDS

WEEK 7:

Your words:

COMPASSION

CALM

INSIGHTS FROM MY WORDS

WEEK 8:

Your words:

CERTAINTY

COMMUNICATION

INSIGHTS FROM MY WORDS

WEEK 9:

Your words:

CREATE

CHANNEL

INSIGHTS FROM MY WORDS

WEEK 10:

Your words:

DETERMINATION

DRIVE

INSIGHTS FROM MY WORDS

WEEK 11:

Your words:

DIRECTION

DIVERSITY

INSIGHTS FROM MY WORDS

WEEK 12:

Your words:

ENTERTAINMENT

ENJOYMENT

INSIGHTS FROM MY WORDS

WEEK 13:

Your words:

ENERGY

EXCITEMENT

INSIGHTS FROM MY WORDS

1ST QUARTER: IDEAS AND INSIGHTS:

WEEK 14:

Your words:

EXCELLENCE

EDUCATION

INSIGHTS FROM MY WORDS

WEEK 15:

Your words:

EXTRA

EXTRAORDINARY

INSIGHTS FROM MY WORDS

WEEK 16:

Your words:

FAME

FORTUNE

INSIGHTS FROM MY WORDS

WEEK 17:

Your words:

FRIEND

FAMILY

INSIGHTS FROM MY WORDS

WEEK 18:

Your words:

FAIRNESS

FORGIVENESS

INSIGHTS FROM MY WORDS

WEEK 19:

Your words:

GREATNESS

GLORY

INSIGHTS FROM MY WORDS

WEEK 20:

Your words:

GRATITUDE

GENEROSITY

INSIGHTS FROM MY WORDS

WEEK 21:

Your words:

GOALS

GROWTH

INSIGHTS FROM MY WORDS

WEEK 22:

Your words:

HOPE

HOME

INSIGHTS FROM MY WORDS

WEEK 23:

Your words:

HELPFUL/HELP

HEALING

INSIGHTS FROM MY WORDS

WEEK 24:

Your words:

HUMOR

INSIGHT

INSIGHTS FROM MY WORDS

WEEK 25:

Your words:

INSPIRATION

INFINITE

INSIGHTS FROM MY WORDS

WEEK 26:

Your words:

JOURNEY

JOY

INSIGHTS FROM MY WORDS

2ND QUARTER: IDEAS AND INSIGHTS:

WEEK 27:

Your words:

JUSTICE

KINDNESS

INSIGHTS FROM MY WORDS

WEEK 28:

Your words:

LIGHT

LOVE

INSIGHTS FROM MY WORDS

WEEK 29:

Your words:

LUCK

LONGEVITY

INSIGHTS FROM MY WORDS

WEEK 30:

Your words:

MAGNIFICENCE

MASTERY

INSIGHTS FROM MY WORDS

WEEK 31:

Your words:

MELODY

NICE

INSIGHTS FROM MY WORDS

WEEK 32:

Your words:

NEW

OPEN

INSIGHTS FROM MY WORDS

WEEK 33:

Your words:

ONWARD

POSITIVE

INSIGHTS FROM MY WORDS

WEEK 34:

Your words:

POWER

PLENTY

INSIGHTS FROM MY WORDS

WEEK 35:

Your words:

PURPOSE

PLAN

INSIGHTS FROM MY WORDS

WEEK 36:

Your words:

PROGRESS

PEACE

INSIGHTS FROM MY WORDS

WEEK 37:

Your words:

QUEST

QUALITY

INSIGHTS FROM MY WORDS

WEEK 38:

Your words:

REJOICE

RELEASE

INSIGHTS FROM MY WORDS

WEEK 39:

Your words:

RELAX

RECREATION

INSIGHTS FROM MY WORDS

3ʳᴰ QUARTER: IDEAS AND INSIGHTS

WEEK 40:

Your words:

RELATIONSHIPS

REUNION

INSIGHTS FROM MY WORDS

WEEK 41:

Your words:

REBIRTH

SERENDIPITY

INSIGHTS FROM MY WORDS

WEEK 42:

Your words:

STRENGTH

SUCCESS

INSIGHTS FROM MY WORDS

WEEK 43:

Your words:

SEARCH

SMILE

INSIGHTS FROM MY WORDS

WEEK 44:

Your words:

SELF-AWARENESS

SELF-KNOWLEDGE

INSIGHTS FROM MY WORDS

WEEK 45:

Your words:

SUNSHINE

TENDERNESS

INSIGHTS FROM MY WORDS

WEEK 46:

Your words:

TRUTH

TRUST

INSIGHTS FROM MY WORDS

WEEK 47:

Your words:

UNITY

UNION

INSIGHTS FROM MY WORDS

WEEK 48:

Your words:

UNIVERSAL

VALUE

INSIGHTS FROM MY WORDS

WEEK 49:

Your words:

VIRTUE

WORTH/WORTHINESS

INSIGHTS FROM MY WORDS

WEEK 50:

Your words:

WILL

WIN

INSIGHTS FROM MY WORDS

WEEK 51:

Your words:

WELCOME

YES

INSIGHTS FROM MY WORDS

WEEK 52:

Your words:

YOUTHFULNESS

ZEST & ZENITH

INSIGHTS FROM MY WORDS

4TH QUARTER: IDEAS AND INSIGHTS

A YEAR FROM A-Z: IDEAS AND INSIGHTS

ABOUT THE AUTHOR

GINI GRAHAM SCOTT, Ph.D., J.D., is a nationally known writer, consultant, speaker, and seminar leader, specializing in business and work relationships, professional and personal development, social trends, and popular culture. She has published over 50 books with major publishers. She has worked with dozens of clients on memoirs, self-help, popular business books, and film scripts. Writing samples are at www.ginigrahamscott.com and www.changemakerspublishingandwriting.com. She is a Huffington Post regular columnist, commenting on social trends, business, and everyday life at www.huffingtonpost.com/gini-graham-scott.

She is the founder of Changemakers Publishing, featuring books on work, business, psychology, social trends, and self-help. It has published over 150 print, e-books, and audiobooks. She has licensed several dozen books for foreign sales, including the UK, Russia, Korea, Spain, and Japan.

She has received national media exposure for her books, including appearances on *Good Morning America, Oprah,* and *CNN*.

Her books on business relationships and professional development include:

Mind Power: Picture Your Way to Success)
The Empowered Mind: How to Harness the Force Within You
Affirmations
Turn Your Dreams into Reality
Resolving Conflict (

Scott is also active in a number of community and business groups, including the Lafayette, Pleasant Hill, and Danville Chambers of Commerce. She is a graduate of the prestigious Leadership Contra Costa program, is a member of two B2B groups in Danville and Walnut Creek, and a BNI member. She is the organizer of six Meetup groups in the film and publishing industries with over 5000 members in Los Angeles and the San Francisco Bay Area. She does workshops and seminars on the topics of her books.

She received her Ph.D. from the University of California, Berkeley, and her J.D. from the University of San Francisco Law School. She has received several MAs at Cal State University, East Bay, including her latest in Communication.

CHANGEMAKERS PUBLISHING
3527 Mt. Diablo Blvd., #273
Lafayette, CA 94549
changemakers@pacbell.net . (925) 385-0608
www.changemakerspublishingandwriting.com

www.ingramcontent.com/pod-product-compliance
Lightning Source LLC
Chambersburg PA
CBHW081351080526
44588CB00016B/2453